LEARN TO TRADE
MOMENTUM STOCKS

2ND EDITION

MATTHEW R. KRATTER

WWW.TRADER.UNIVERSITY

CONTENTS

For my children

DISCLAIMER

Neither Little Cash Machines LLC, nor any of its directors, officers, shareholders, personnel, representatives, agents, or independent contractors (collectively, the "Operator Parties") are licensed financial advisers, registered investment advisers, or registered broker-dealers. None of the Operator Parties are providing investment, financial, legal, or tax advice, and nothing in this book or at www.Trader.University (henceforth, "the Site") should be construed as such by you. This book and the Site should be used as educational tools only and are not replacements for professional investment advice. The full disclaimer can be found at the end of this book.

YOUR FREE GIFT

Thanks for purchasing my book!

As a way of showing my appreciation, I've created a **Free Video Tutorial** for you.

I want you to be able to screen for momentum stocks on your own.

And I want you to have a copy of my trading chart, which will show you exactly when to buy and sell a momentum stock.

There was no way to include this video material in a written book, so I created this free video tutorial for you.

In it, you will learn:

- How to find the best momentum stocks

- How to set up a trading chart that will give you buy and sell signals for any momentum stock

This video tutorial will show you exactly how to get started using the momentum stocks trading strategy:

>>>Tap Here to Get the Free Video Tutorial<<<

Or simply go to:

http://www.trader.university/momentum/

THE POWER OF TREND FOLLOWING

In this book, you will learn a powerful strategy for trading momentum stocks.

There are many stock trading strategies that work for a while, and then stop working.

Momentum is not one of them.

Momentum was first documented as a stock market anomaly in the early 1990's.

And it's still working.

Once you learn how to trade momentum stocks, you will have a tool in your trader toolbox that you can use for the rest of your life.

So what exactly is a "momentum stock"?

It is any stock that keeps moving in a certain direction (whether up or down) for an extended period of time.

During the dot-com boom of the late 1990's, Yahoo, eBay, Oracle, and Cisco were momentum stocks.

They went straight up for a couple of years, and then straight down even more quickly from 2000-2002. These stocks had momentum on the upside and on the downside as well.

Buy and hold investors who held these stocks over this period saw their wealth soar, and then plummet.

As you might guess, a buy and hold investment strategy should never be used with momentum stocks.

There is a better way—one that is much less stressful.

In this book, you will learn that better way.

It's called "trend following."

You probably have heard the expression "the trend is your friend."

But you may not have realized just how powerful trend-following can be.

John W. Henry used it to earn enough money to buy the Boston Red Sox.

Studies have shown that there have always been trends in the markets, even going back hundreds of years.

This makes sense, since human nature is a constant.

Trend following seeks to profit from this collective behavior of market participants, who move into and out of the market, driven by vast alternating waves of fear and greed.

In a trend-following strategy, you only buy stocks that are rising, and you sell them immediately if they begin to fall.

You don't try to predict the future.

You simply use the price action itself to tell you what you should be doing.

As you will see, there are precise ways to measure this price action, so that you will never need to second-guess yourself.

The trading rules that you will learn in this book are quite simple.

You will learn exactly when to buy a stock, when to take profits, and when to exit a losing trade.

You will learn how to size a position.

And most importantly, you will learn what pond to fish in, if you want to catch the best momentum stocks.

I've been trading for over 20 years.

I've learned what works in the markets-- and what does not.

Trend-following is a strategy that works extremely well with momentum stocks.

Even better, it does not require you to be glued to your computer monitor all day long.

You will not need multiple charts, news feeds, or dozens of indicators.

You will never suffer from "analysis paralysis," where one indicator is telling you to buy while another indicator is telling you to sell.

You will have the freedom to put on a position, and then leave your computer and go to the beach for the day.

As a long-term trader, you will enjoy a much higher quality of life than a short-term trader.

As you will see, trend following is a simple, elegant method of extracting wealth from the markets.

For example, the trend-following system that you are about to learn bought Tesla (TSLA) in December 2012 and held it until July 2013 for a gain of 300%.

It bought Apple (AAPL) in May 2003 and held it until January 2005, for a gain of 300%.

And then a few years later, it did it again, buying Apple in May 2009 and holding it until February 2012 for another gain of 300%.

Read on, to learn the exact strategy that you can use to find the next Tesla or Apple.

2

WHERE TO FISH FOR MOMENTUM STOCKS

So where should we look to find the next Tesla or Apple?

The short answer:

Young companies that are rapidly growing their sales (revenues).

There is no point in trying to trend-follow the stock of a slow-growing company like Coca-Cola.

Coke has grown its revenues only 4.5% annually for the past 5 years.

By contrast, Apple has grown its revenues by over 36% annually for the past 5 years.

Coke is a fairly predictable, slow-growing company.

Not so, Apple or Tesla or Facebook or Netflix.

For these fast-growing companies, future revenues and earnings are quite difficult to predict.

As a result, their stocks are volatile.

Money flows in and out of these stocks in great waves that we can ride.

As we said, the best momentum stocks are associated with companies that are rapidly growing their revenues.

I like to group these companies into 2 main buckets:

1. New Technology Companies (NTC)
2. Formula Companies

New Technology Companies (NTC)

NTC are companies that are doing new things.

They are inventing or popularizing new technologies, like a Facebook or a Tesla.

They are often in high-tech industries like software, information technology, biotechnology, hardware, or other engineering-intensive areas.

Because they are disrupting the status quo (Tesla with its

electric cars), or creating new markets (like Apple did for the smart phone), they are often able to grow sales quite rapidly.

Of course over time, new technology becomes the status quo, sales growth slows, and the company either becomes an established blue-chip company, is bought by another company, or goes out of business.

Microsoft, Oracle, and Cisco were momentum stocks in the late 1990's, but now are dividend-paying stalwarts.

If a company pays a dividend, it is usually not a good candidate for the momentum stocks strategy.

That being said, if the company pays a dividend and continues to grow its revenues rapidly (like Apple), it might still qualify.

Formula Companies

Formula Companies invent a successful formula (like burgers and fries served under Golden Arches), and then replicate that formula across the country-- and eventually around the world.

These include lots of consumer, retail, or restaurant stocks like McDonald's, Home Depot, Starbucks, Panera Bread, Tractor Supply, and Ulta Beauty.

As in the case of New Technology Companies, all Formula

Companies eventually saturate their consumer markets (how many Starbucks can you really have on one street?).

Their sales growth slows, and the company eventually becomes another dividend-paying blue chip.

Many years ago, McDonald's was a good momentum stock, but no longer.

For both NTC and Formula Stocks, it is important to see rapidly growing revenues.

There are many companies that are doing new and interesting things, but until it shows up in the revenues, we are not interested.

We want to see revenues, and we want to see them growing rapidly.

What qualifies as rapid revenue growth?

To answer this question, let's take a look at Facebook, obviously a New Technology Company:

Facebook	Revenues (millions)		YoY rev growth	3 yr avg rev growth
2008	$	272		
2009	$	777	186%	
2010	$	1,974	154%	
2011	$	3,711	88%	143%
2012	$	5,089	37%	93%
2013	$	7,872	55%	60%
2014	$	12,466	58%	50%
2015	$	17,928	44%	52%
2016	$	27,638	54%	52%

Between 2008 and 2016, Facebook grew its revenues anywhere between 37% and 186% annually.

Three-year average revenue growth ranged between 50% and 143%.

This is clearly extraordinary sales growth, made possible by Facebook's technical innovation and global reach.

Now let's turn to Ulta Beauty, a Formula Company:

Ulta Beauty		Revenues (thousands)		YoY rev growth	3 yr avg rev growth
2009	$		1,222,771		
2010	$		1,454,838	19%	
2011	$		1,776,151	22%	
2012	$		2,220,256	25%	22%
2013	$		2,670,573	20%	22%
2014	$		3,241,369	21%	22%
2015	$		3,924,116	21%	21%
2016	$		4,854,737	24%	22%

Between 2009 and 2016, Ulta grew its revenues anywhere between 21% and 22% annually.

While not as high as Facebook, this revenue growth is still impressive.

Like all Formula Companies, Ulta tested its key selling strategies in a few stores, discovered what worked best, and then proceeded to roll out the strategy nationwide.

It currently operates 974 stores across the U.S.

We had previously asked, what qualifies as rapid revenue growth?

Having looked at Facebook and Ulta as typical examples, we are now in a position to answer that question.

For a trend-following candidate, we want to see annual revenue growth greater than 20%, as a rule of thumb.

Three-year average revenue growth should also be north of 20% ideally, though this can be a lagging indicator.

These are not a hard and fast rules, so we shouldn't quibble if we see annual revenue growth of 19%, or if growth temporarily falls off during a recession.

But good momentum stocks will often have revenue growth rates north of 30%, 50%, or even 100% in their early years.

For example, Tesla grew its revenues at 102% in 2012, at 387% in 2013, and at 59% in 2014.

To summarize, what pond should we be fishing in to find good momentum stocks?

The ideal candidate:

- is a New Technology Company, or Formula Company
- has an annual revenue growth rate north of 20%.

Do you want to learn how to find stocks like these that have high revenue growth?

I show you how to do it in my **Free Video Tutorial** which you can get here:

www.trader.university/momentum

I like to keep a list of stocks like these on my desk, so that I can check them every evening, to see if a buy signal has been triggered.

It is now time to learn exactly what constitutes a buy signal.

3

THE EXACT TRADING RULES: WHEN TO BUY, AND WHEN TO SELL

Buy stocks that go up; if they don't go up, don't buy them.

WILL ROGERS

W e now have a list of (high revenue growth) stocks that could turn into momentum stocks.

Now we just need to wait for the market to tell us when to trade.

We do not want to tie up our money in a stock that has not yet demonstrated that it actually has momentum!

Instead, we need to wait for a buy signal to occur.

When to Buy

A buy signal is triggered:

1. When stock's 50-day moving average crosses over ("closes higher than") its 200-day moving average; and
2. Only if the stock is currently trading above its 50-day moving average when this crossover occurs.

When both of these conditions are met, you buy the stock the next morning when the market opens.

You can use a "market on open" order if the stock is liquid, or simply wait 5 minutes to see where the stock is trading, and then enter using a market or limit order.

We are looking to capture a big move, so it doesn't really matter if our entry price is $0.50 higher or lower.

To calculate the 50-day moving average, you add up a stock's daily closing price for each of the last 50 trading days (i.e. don't count weekends), and divide by 50:

(price 50 days ago + price 49 days ago + price 48 days + . . . + price yesterday + closing price today) divided by 50.

To calculate the 200-day moving average, you do the same

thing: add up the stock's closing price for each of the last 200 trading days, and divide by 200.

Fortunately, you do not need to do this by hand. There are free websites that will do these calculations for you and chart them like this:

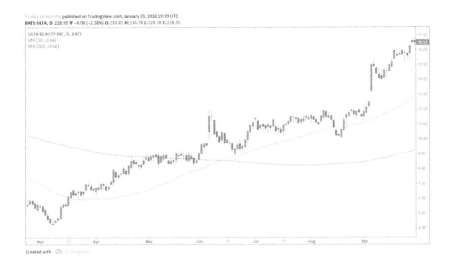

In this chart, the blue line is the 50-day moving average, and the red line is the 200-day moving average.

If you are reading this in a black-and-white format, the blue line is the line that starts on the bottom and then moves above ("crosses over) the red line.

You can get your own copy of this chart here:

www.trader.university/momentum

This indicator is extremely simple, but don't underestimate its power.

Every great run in a stock like Apple, Facebook, or Tesla began with a moving average crossover.

Sometimes the media even reports on it.

This is truly one of those treasures that is hidden in plain view!

When the 50-day moving average crosses over the 200-day moving average, it indicates that an uptrend has begun.

Since we are trend-followers, we will buy the stock here and ride the trend for as long as we can.

When to Sell

There are 3 possible signals that it is time to exit our position:

1. **If the stock falls 15% from your entry price, sell the stock immediately.** This is our emergency stop loss, and prevents a small loss from becoming a big loss. A stock should not fall this much at the beginning of a strong uptrend, and so we do not want to stick around. Many readers have asked me: why such a wide stop-loss? The answer is that momentum stocks tend to be extremely volatile. Even daily moves of 5% or more are not uncommon,

and so we need to have a fairly wide stop, in order to ensure that we are not shaken out by the natural volatility of the stock.

2. **If the 50-day moving average closes BELOW the 200-day moving average, sell the stock the next morning when the market opens. The trend is now over and it is dangerous to remain holding the stock!** After a long trend has occurred, this will be the signal that it is time to take profits. Sometimes a trend will be weak, and the 50-day moving average will close below the 200-day moving average not long after you buy the stock. Exit the stock immediately, take your loss, and move on.

3. **If the stock rises 300% from your entry price, exit the stock completely and take profits.** Some stocks will go on to rally another 200%, while some stocks will start crashing the next day. I have found that a 300% move is the sweet spot that allows you to capture most of the uptrend and book it as a profit, while not getting greedy and overstaying your welcome at the party.

You can see that we risk 15% to make 300%.

In other words, one winning trade will pay for 20 losing trades.

That is a great risk-reward ratio.

Even if you are stopped out of a trade 90% of the time, you can still expect to make 16.50% per trade on average over the long term.

As George Soros is fond of saying:

It's not whether you're right or wrong that's important,
but how much money you make when you're right and
how much lose when you're wrong.

We've now discussed the importance of stop losses and low risk-reward ratios.

In the next chapter, we will cover the third pillar of risk management-- position sizing.

4

HOW TO SIZE YOUR POSITIONS AND MANAGE RISK

Now it is time to walk through an actual trade, in order to see how to size a position.

It is back in 2009, and Apple is on our momentum watch-list because it is a New Technology Company (NTC), and it has been growing its revenues north of 20% annually.

Then on 13 May 2009, the 50-day moving average closes over the 200-day moving average.

On this day, the stock is also trading above its 50-day moving average, and so a buy signal is triggered:

- Closing price of Apple stock (split-adjusted): 17.07
- 50-day moving average: 16.13
- 200-day moving average: 16.07

Let's pretend that you want to place this trade for your account.

We make the following assumptions:

- You have $10,000 in your trading account.
- You want to risk 2% of your account on each trade, or $200.
- You assume that you will be able to enter the stock close to 17.07, so you set your stop loss 15% below that. To calculate this, simply multiply 17.07 by 0.85, to get 14.50 as your stop loss.

Now use the following formula to calculate how many shares you should buy:

number of shares to buy = (account size times the percentage risked on each trade) / (entry price - stop loss)

= ($10,000 x 0.02) / (17.07 - 14.50)

= 77.82 shares, which we will round up to 80 shares.

So on 14 May 2009 (the day after the moving cross-over occurred), you put in a market on open order to buy 80 shares of Apple.

You are filled at the opening price of 17.11 on 80 shares.

Now that you own the stock, you can recalculate your stop

loss to be 15% below your actual purchase price of 17.11. This sets your stop loss at 14.54.

Now it is important to sit on your hands and do nothing.

Don't read any news about Apple.

Don't hang out on the message boards or in the forums, or let people influence your opinion of Apple one way or another.

It's best not to discuss the trade with your friends or family.

You don't want to get too bearish or too bullish.

You are allowed to start watching the stock when it gets close to your stop loss level of 14.54.

But don't actually enter a stop loss order into the market.

Instead, set up a price alert with your broker.

Most brokers will allow you to put in a price alert that is triggered when a stock hits a certain price.

If your stop loss is at 14.54, you can put in a price alert at 14.70 or so.

Then when the stock hits 14.70, you will receive a text or email.

Then (and only then) you can start watching your stock trade and prepare to exit.

Exit immediately if the stock touches your stop loss price during regular market hours.

You are also free to put in a sell limit order that is 300% above your entry price.

To calculate this, take your entry price and multiply it by 4. In this case, 17.11 times 4 equals 68.44.

Feel free to put in a sell limit order at 68.44.

If you use a GTC ("good til cancelled") limit order, be sure to cancel it, if you end up exiting the stock earlier.

Every evening you are allowed to check to see if the 50-day moving average has closed below the 200-day moving average.

If it has crossed over, you must sell the stock immediately when the market opens the next morning.

That's it!

Now fast-forward to 9 February 2012.

On that day, your sell limit order is filled, and you end up selling the stock for 68.44.

You have now captured 51.33 points in Apple (68.44 minus 17.11 equals 51.33) on 80 shares for a profit of $4,106.40 (51.33 times 80).

After commissions of $4.95 to enter and $4.95 to exit, you have made $4,096.50 in a $10,000 account, for a return of almost 41%.

Remember that you risked only 2% of your account on this trade, for a 41% return.

A more conservative trader might have risked only 1%, and received a 20% return.

An aggressive trader might have risked 10%, and received roughly a 200% return.

If you are just starting out, it might make sense to spread your capital over 15 stocks.

So if you are trading a $15,000 dollar account, every time you get a buy signal, you allocate $1,000 to that stock.

If the stock immediately drops 15% and you are stopped out, you have just lost $150 or 1% of your trading account.

That is a very manageable loss, and will enable you to become comfortable trading with real money.

As your comfort and capital increase, you will be in a position to make more aggressive bets on each subsequent buy signal.

5

HOW TO MILK A STOCK FOR PROFITS OVER MANY YEARS

Let's now examine a single momentum stock over many years to see how the trading strategy would have traded it.

This will be a great way to see how the system deals with both winning and losing trades.

I've already discussed Ulta Beauty (ULTA), and its high revenue growth.

It is clearly an amazing company ("Formula Company") with a powerful growth strategy.

And yet the market had a difficult time trying to figure out how to value it (as is often the case with high-growth companies).

Ulta went public on 25 October 2007, just a few months before the financial crisis hit.

It proceeded to sell off immediately, as the bear market hit and insider selling pummeled the stock.

In fact, Ulta fell from a high of 35.63 all the way down to 4.11.

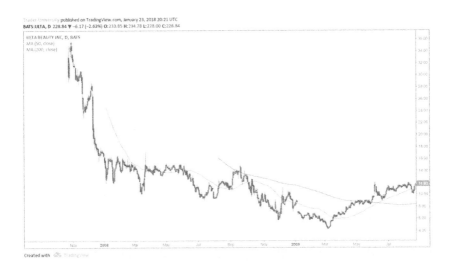

That's a loss of over 88% in just a year and a half.

Strangely, at the same time, the business itself was continuing to produce excellent results.

Despite the recession, Ulta's revenues were growing rapidly every year.

The bear market ended in March 2009, and Ulta's stock began to recover along with the rest of the stock market.

The stock more than doubled from 4.11 to over 10.

And yet, it was still not time to buy.

Finally, our patience was rewarded:

On 12 June 2009, the 50-day moving average closed above the 200-day moving average (in case you are reading this in black-and-white, the 50-day moving average is the line that begins on the bottom and ends up on top):

Since the stock was also trading above its 50-day moving average, it was now time to buy the stock, the next morning on the open.

We were filled at 10.39 on June 15, and we set our mental stop loss 15% lower at 8.83.

Now it was time to wait and watch.

Unfortunately, Ulta immediately began to sell off.

It got as low as 8.90 (just 7 cents away from our stop loss), before beginning to recover.

As our confidence returned, we set our profit target at +300%

10.39 (our entry price) times 4 is 41.56

We entered a GTC ("good til cancelled") sell limit order at 41.56.

Now it was again time to wait.

A year passed.

And then another 7 months.

Finally on 9 February 2011, ULTA traded at 41.56 and we sold our stock for a 300% profit.

Unfortunately (or fortunately, depending on your perspective), ULTA continued to rally for another 2 years.

The 50-day moving average stayed above the 200-day moving average the whole time.

By the time the 50-day moving average crossed below the 200-day moving average (on 15 March 2013), the stock was up over 600% from our original June 2009 entry point.

This brings us to a very important point.

Taking profits at a 300% gain is usually the right thing to do.

It never feels that bad to put a lot of money into your pocket.

That being said, if you wish to maximize total trading profits over an entire lifetime, you should always wait for the moving-average crossover before you take profits.

Some people like to bank money now.

Some like to maximize profits over the long term.

Either path is fine, and will depend on your own personal psychology and risk tolerance.

The nice thing about booking a 300% gain when you are first starting out is that it "pays" for your next 20 trading losses (where you get stopped out at 15% each time).

Most of you should probably exit at a 300% gain while you are learning the trading strategy.

But if you were a profit maximizer, you waited for the moving average crossover in ULTA and exited at the open at 73.61 on 18 March 2013.

You made 608%.

Either way, you were now in cash and waiting for the next signal.

You didn't have to wait long.

On 5 July 2013, the 50-day moving average closed above the 200-day moving average yet again.

And so we bought ULTA on the open the next day (July 8) at 100.15.

We set our stop loss at 85.13, which is 15% lower than our entry price.

Things were looking good again:

ULTA began to rally and got as high as 132.

We were up almost 32% on our trade.

And then something terrible happened:

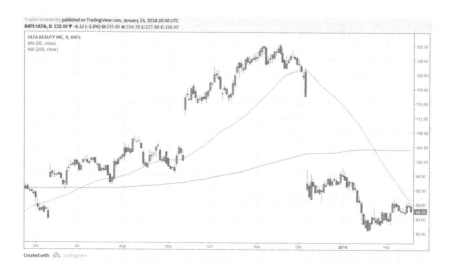

Following a bad quarterly earnings report, the stock tanked overnight.

After being up 32% on the trade, you were now down more than 5%.

This time, the stock did not make a rapid recovery.

Instead, it continued to sell off until it hit our stop loss price of 85.13.

We exited immediately and took our 15% loss on 15 January 2014.

It's important to remember that when trading momentum stocks, **you will have losses.**

There is no way around that.

What matters is how you react.

Do you exit at your stop loss level, or do you ignore it and "hope" for a recovery?

When trading any strategy, you will have winning trades and losing trades.

What really matters, as we quoted George Soros above, is how much money you make when you win, and how much money you lose when you lose.

By sticking with stocks with high revenue growth, and faithfully following the trading signals, you will put the odds firmly in your favor.

After we exited ULTA at our stop loss, a series of losing days managed to drag the 50-day moving average below the 200-day moving average (27 January 2014):

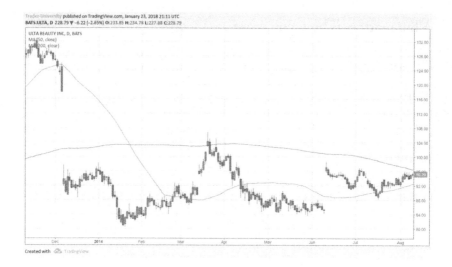

You can see here how the 50-day moving average is definitely a lagging indicator.

By the time it crossed below the 200-day moving average, we had already been stopped out (near the lows) and the stock had already begun to recover.

It is frustrating to see that the stock even rallied back up to our entry price of 100.

"If we had just held on, we would not have had to take that loss."

It is very important not to think this way.

For every time that a stock recovers, there are two more times that a stock keeps selling off-- and even goes down to zero.

Stick with the trading signals (and your stop losses), and don't try to second guess them.

Learn to take losses and move on.

It's the only way that you can develop the psychology of a professional trader.

Fortunately, we did not have to wait long for our next trade.

On 3 September 2014, the 50-day moving average closed above the 200-day moving average.

On 4 September 2014, we bought the stock at the open at 99.42, and set our mental stop loss at 99.42 times 0.85 or 84.50.

The stock immediately began to rally.

And it continued to go up for many months:

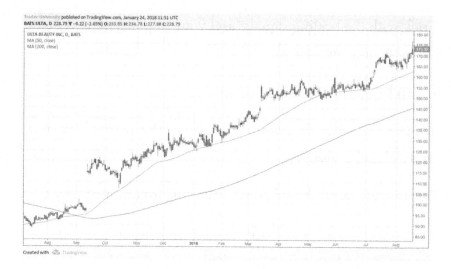

That's not to say that there weren't any scary moments along the way.

Just look at what happened one day:

The previous day, the stock had closed at 162.57 (up from our entry of 99.42).

The next day, the stock opens at 143.00 (down 12% from the previous day's close), and proceeds to sell off all the way down to 120.38.

By the end of the day, it had rallied back up to 158.72, nearly back to the previous day's close.

If you were watching the stock do this during market hours, you probably nearly had a heart attack.

However, if you were at the beach, you never even noticed.

And with your price alert set near 84.50 (your stop loss level), your initial capital was protected.

In the following weeks and months, the stock recovered and went on to hit many new highs.

200.

250.

300.

All the while, the 50-day moving average stayed above the 200-day moving average:

At the far right of this chart, we can see that the 50-day moving average finally closed below the 200-day moving average on 15 August 2017.

We sold the stock on 16 August 2017 at the open at 238.02 for a 139% gain.

Not a bad trade, but certainly not a multibagger.

But that's OK, because we stuck to our discipline and following our trading strategy rules.

You can see how much a stock can retrace from its highs before an exit is triggered.

In this case, ULTA retraced from a high of 314.86 all the way down to 238 before we exited.

Could we have locked in profits sooner?

Certainly.

On the other hand, if you always lock in profits sooner, you will miss out on the 300-600% gainers that we have seen.

The choice is yours.

Most amateur traders sell their winners too early, and hold on to their losers too long.

The point of this trading strategy is to help you to fight these very natural (but unfortunately money-losing) urges.

We've already looked at Facebook's amazing revenue growth.

Let's see now how we would have traded its price action.

Much like Ulta, Facebook (FB) came public in an IPO, and immediately sold off hard:

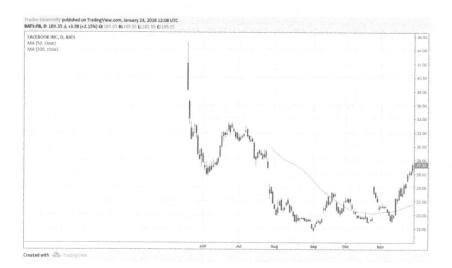

Once again, it paid to wait for the moving average crossover before entering the stock.

That crossover came on 5 August 2013:

Since the stock was also trading above the 50-day moving average, we entered the stock the next day on the open at 39.11, and set our mental stop loss 15% lower at 33.24.

We set our profit target at 39.11 times 4 equals 156.44.

Facebook continued to rally for many months, with the 50-day moving average always remaining above the 200-day moving average.

Like Ulta, there were some crazy days when the stock sold off hard intraday and then recovered:

Since a moving-average crossover did not occur, we held on for dear life.

This was made somewhat easier by our good entry price.

If a stock falls from 99 down to 72, it hurts.

But if you own the stock at 39 (as we did), it is much easier.

It almost feels as if you are playing with the house's money at that point.

Facebook recovered from this temporary blip, and continued to rally.

Finally, on 6 January 2017, the 50-day moving average closed below the 200-day moving average:

We exited the stock the next day on the market open at 123.55, for a total gain of 216%.

You can see in the chart the kind of fake-out that occurred.

The 50-day moving average dipped below the 200-day

moving average for just a short time, before crossing back above it on 31 January 2017.

At that point, the stock was trading around 130.

We had just sold it at 123.55.

So we felt like idiots.

Nevertheless, we followed the system and bought back again the next day at the open at 132.25.

Fortunately, Facebook did not disappoint.

It rallied past 150.

And then past 180.

As I write these words, the trade is still open and looks like this:

I still own the stock, and will not sell it until the 50-day moving average crosses below the 200-day moving average.

Or until I hit my profit target of 132.25 times 4 equals 529.

It seems hard to believe that the stock could go up that much, but I've seen it happen many times before.

So, I'll just continue to trade the system and see what happens.

In the meantime, I know that the next bear market is coming.

In the next chapter, I'll teach you how to survive when the inevitable "bad times" come.

6

HOW TO SHORT MOMENTUM STOCKS

Y ou often hear that it is impossible to predict a bear market.

This is, of course, true.

But fortunately, in trend following, we are not trying to predict anything.

We are simply following trends—on the way up, and on the way down as well.

We cannot predict the future, but we can react to its gradual unfolding.

Bear markets do not come out of nowhere.

In fact, every bear market begins with many stocks' 50-day

moving averages crossing below their 200-day moving averages.

Major stock indices will also see their 50-day moving averages cross below their 200-day moving averages.

While we cannot predict a bear market, we can certainly protect ourselves against one by exiting a long position when a stock's 50-day moving average crosses below its 200-day moving average.

If we are aggressive traders, we can even profit from such a downturn, by going short.

As I mentioned in the first chapter, growth stocks tend to have strong momentum on the way up, and even stronger momentum on the way down.

A stock that ran from 10 to 200 over three years might come crashing back down to 10 in a matter of 12 months.

In fact, many momentum stocks end up giving back all or most of their entire advance.

For example, in the bear market of 2000-2002, many momentum stocks declined 80-90% from their highs.

Near the end of a momentum stock's long uptrend, it will frequently be trading at a truly irrational price/earnings multiple.

No amount of business success or growth will ever be able to justify such a multiple.

On the way up, no one cares, because everyone is making money.

But when the stock's upward momentum begins to slow, or even reverse, investors will once again turn to the stock's valuation, realize how crazy it is, and decide to sell their shares.

This selling helps to accelerate the stock's downward move.

Cisco Systems (CSCO) is a perfect example of this dynamic at work:

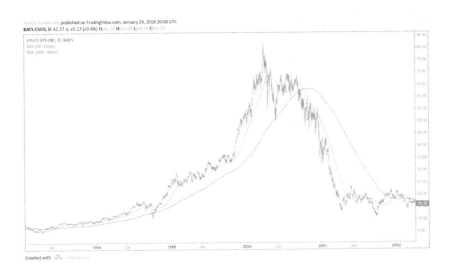

For CSCO, the 50-day moving average crossed above the 200-day moving average on 27 June 1997 when the stock was trading at a split-adjusted price of 7.39.

The stock proceeded to run for the next two and a half years, topping out at split-adjusted high of 82.00 and a P/E of almost 174!

The 50-day moving average finally crossed back below the 200-day moving average on 4 October 2000, at a split-adjusted closing price of 58.56.

When this happened, the stock promptly fell another 86%, finally bottoming out at split-adjusted low of 8.12 on 8 October 2002.

After a tremendous run of over 1000%, the stock retraced almost completely.

Almost everyone was surprised both by how far the stock rallied, and by how far it retraced.

Everyone, that is, except for the trend-followers who captured the majority of the move up and the move down.

So how does one short a momentum stock?

First, never be foolish enough to short a momentum stock until the 50-day moving average has closed below the 200-day moving average.

Many otherwise very smart traders have lost their shirts trying to short stocks like Cisco on the way up.

The stock was certainly overvalued, but it kept going up.

Second, look for stocks that have had tremendous run-ups, but whose revenue growth is beginning to slow.

The market is very quick to punish high-flying stocks whose growth begins to slow.

Shorting stocks can be quite risky, and is therefore not for everyone.

That being said, if you are able to bear the risks, the remainder of the chapter will teach you how.

To short a stock, it is first necessary for the stock to be available to "borrow" from your broker.

If you cannot find a broker who will lend you the stock from its inventory, it is impossible to short the stock (one can do it synthetically with options, but that is a whole other story, that I may discuss in a future book).

Once you have been able to borrow shares of the stock, you sell the shares into the market ("sell short" is the broker's order that you'll want to use).

At the end of your trade, you will buy back the shares ("buy to cover") and deliver them back to your broker.

This process of borrowing and delivery is usually automated, and is much easier than it sounds.

If the stock has declined, you will have made money.

If the stock has gone up, you will have lost money.

In short selling, the key is to "sell high" and "buy low"--in that order!

Short selling a momentum stock is further complicated by the fact that it can be tricky to figure out where to set your stop.

It is usually best to set a fairly wide stop of 10-20% (or even more) from entry.

Thus, if you short a stock at 100 and are using a 20% stop, you will exit your short if the stock trades at 120.

The problem with shorting is that your maximum profit is 100%.

For example, if you short a stock at 100 and it goes to zero, you have just made 100% (before commissions, which are minimal).

Unfortunately, you had to risk 10-20% (your stop loss) to put on this trade.

At a 20% stop, **you are basically risking 1 dollar to make 5 dollars.**

On the long-side of trend following in Chapter 3, we were risking 15% to make 300%.

In other words, **we were risking 1 dollar to make 20 dollars.**

The risk-reward ratio of shorting is far inferior to that of going long.

For this reason, many traders will go on vacation at the beginning of a bear market.

They will have made their money in the preceding bull market, and will see no reason to endure the stress of a bear market, where the risks far out-weigh the rewards.

To summarize, for those hardy souls who want to trade momentum stocks on the downside, there are 3 things to look for:

1. The 50-day moving average needs to close below the 200-day moving average for the stock in question.
2. The stock needs to have had a long run-up.
3. And preferably, the stock needs to show signs of slowing revenue or earnings growth.

In the latter category, a stock will often have a revenue or earnings miss.

It will gap down sharply when it reports slowing growth, or revenues or earnings that are below the market's expectations.

A textbook example of a successful short is the shoemaker Crocs (CROX) in late 2007.

The stock had had a long run-up, from its IPO in February 2006, all the way to October 31, 2007.

On that day, after the market closed, Crocs reported disappointing earnings and projected 2008 revenue growth that fell short of the market's expectations.

How do we know that the earnings report fell short of Wall Street's high expectations, even if we don't know how to read an earnings transcript?

Simply based on the stock's reaction.

It fell in the after-hours market and closed down 36% the following day.

Now most people would find it quite difficult to short a stock that had already fallen 36%.

But we trend followers know that the time to short a momentum stock is when its momentum has sharply reversed, and not a moment before.

Then on 2 January 2008, the 50-day moving average closed below the 200-day moving average and the stock closed at 37.90.

If you had gone short the following day at the market open at 38.00 and set your stop at 10%, you would have been able to ride the stock all the way down from 38.00 to 3.02 (which is where the stock was trading when the 50-day moving average finally crossed back above the 200-day moving average).

You would have made 92% on this trade, and risked only 10%.

That is about as good as shorting can get.

There is one more thing that you should know about shorting momentum stocks.

When you borrow shares of a stock from your broker that you wish to short, you will need to pay a fee that is based on how long you borrow the shares for.

When many people are trying to short a certain stock, that

stock will be on the "hard-to-borrow list"—meaning that it can be expensive to borrow the shares from a broker.

Sometimes these fees can be as high as 100% annualized.

This means that if the stock that you have shorted goes to zero in one year, you make 100%, but need to pay your broker 100% (because the stock was hard-to-borrow and you held it for 1 year at an annualized 100% borrow rate).

High borrowing costs make it extremely important to time your entry correctly (using the 50/200 moving average cross-over method that we have discussed).

As we have seen, the stock needs to fall faster than your borrow rate, or you will end up losing money even if the trade itself makes money.

For example, if you have borrowed the stock at a 100% annualized borrow rate, and it falls 50% in 3 months, you are still OK.

You make 50% on the stock short, and only have to pay 25% in borrowing costs (100%/12 months times 3 months= 25%), for a net return of 50% - 25% = 25%.

Even worse, when you are short a stock, it is possible for the broker to ask for the shares back at any time.

If this occurs (and it almost always occurs at the worst possible time!), you will need to cover your short (buy back the shares in the open market) wherever it happens to be trading that day.

When shorts are forced to cover by their brokers, the stock will typically rally significantly, so that you will probably be buying back your shares at a loss.

Therefore my best advice is this:

When you are first starting out, trade your momentum stocks from the long side only.

Exit your long position when the 50-day moving average crosses below the 200-day moving average, and don't try to get short.

You will make plenty of money on the long side, and avoid all of the complications and stresses associated with shorting a stock.

When a bear market begins, take all of your chips off the table and go hang out on a tropical beach somewhere.

You'll be glad that you did.

7

HOW TO GET STARTED TODAY

We've covered a lot of ground in this book.

I hope that you are ready to take this information and use it to start making money for yourself trading momentum stocks.

Be sure to consult your financial advisor and tax advisor first, and if all looks good, just get started.

The best way to learn about trading is to start doing it.

Open a paper trading account (just google "paper trading account brokers"), and you will be able to trade without risking any real money.

Once you get more comfortable, you can start trading with real money.

Begin with very small positions, and then slowly increase them as your capital (and your confidence!) increases.

There's no better way to learn than simply by doing.

And I'm here to help you on your journey.

If you have questions, or just want to say hi, write to me at matt@trader.university

I love to hear from my readers, and I answer every email personally.

I hope that you will find trading momentum stocks to be as rewarding as I have.

Nothing is more exciting than riding a long trend in a momentum stock, and then taking profits.

And it is especially nice to be on the sidelines (or short!) when the momentum stock inevitably comes crashing back down to earth.

Before you go, I'd like to say "thank you" for purchasing this book and reading it all the way to the end.

If you enjoyed this book and found it useful, I'd be very grateful if you'd post an honest review on Amazon.

All that you need to do is to click here and then click on the correct book cover.

Or go to www.trader.university and click on the "Books" tab, and then click on the correct book cover.

Then click the blue link next to the yellow stars that says "customer reviews."

You'll then see a gray button that says "Write a customer review"—click that and you're good to go.

If you would like to learn more ways to make money in the markets, check out my other Kindle books on the next page.

ALSO BY MATTHEW R. KRATTER

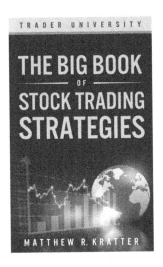

Click here to buy this book on Amazon

Or simply go to www.trader.university and click on the "Books" tab.

Click here to buy this book on Amazon

Or simply go to www.trader.university and click on the "Books" tab.

YOUR FREE GIFT

Thanks for purchasing my book!

As a way of showing my appreciation, I've created a **Free Video Tutorial** for you.

I want you to be able to screen for momentum stocks on your own.

And I want you to have a copy of my trading chart, which will show you exactly when to buy and sell a momentum stock.

There was no way to include this video material in a written book, so I created this free video tutorial for you.

In it, you will learn:

- How to find the best momentum stocks

- How to set up a trading chart that will give you buy and sell signals for any momentum stock

This video tutorial will show you exactly how to get started using the momentum stocks trading strategy:

>>>Tap Here to Get the Free Video Tutorial<<<

Or simply go to:

http://www.trader.university/momentum/

ABOUT THE AUTHOR

Hi there!

My name is Matthew Kratter.

I am the founder of Trader University, and the best-selling author of multiple books on trading and investing.

I have more than 20 years of trading experience, including working at multiple hedge funds.

Most individual traders and investors are at a huge disadvantage when it comes to the markets. Most are unable to invest in hedge funds. Yet, when they trade their own money, they are competing against computer algorithms, math PhD's, and multi-billion dollar hedge funds.

I've been on the inside of many hedge funds. I know how professional traders and investors think and approach the markets. And I am committed to sharing their trading strategies with you in my books and courses.

When I am not trading or writing new books, I enjoy skiing,

hiking, and otherwise hanging out in the Rocky Mountains with my wife, kids, and dogs.

If you enjoyed this book, you may also enjoy my other Kindle titles, which are available here:

http://www.trader.university

Just click on the tab that says "Books."

Or send me an email at matt@trader.university.

I would love to hear from you.

DISCLAIMER

While the author has used his best efforts in preparing this book, he makes no representations or warranties with respect to the accuracy or completeness of the contents of this book and specifically disclaims any implied warranties or merchantability or fitness for a particular purpose. The advice and strategies contained herein may not be suitable for your situation.

You should consult with a legal, financial, tax, or other professional where appropriate.

Neither the publisher nor the author shall be liable for any loss of profit or any other commercial damages, including but not limited to special, incidental, consequential, or other damages.

This book is for educational purposes only. The views expressed are those of the author alone, and should not be taken as expert instruction or commands. The reader is responsible for his or her own actions.

Adherence to all applicable laws and regulations, including international, federal, state, and local laws, is the sole responsibility of the purchaser or reader.

Neither the author nor the publisher assumes any responsibility or liability whatsoever on the behalf of the purchaser or reader of these materials.

Any perceived slight of any individual or organization is purely unintentional.

Past performance is not necessarily indicative of future performance. Forex, futures, stock, and options trading is not appropriate for everyone. There is a substantial risk of loss associated with trading these markets. Losses can and will occur. No system or methodology has ever been developed that can guarantee profits or ensure freedom from losses. Nor will it likely ever be. No representation or implication is being made that using the methodologies or systems or the information contained within this book will generate profits or ensure freedom from losses. The information contained in this book is for educational purposes only and should NOT be taken as investment advice. Examples presented here are not solicitations to buy or sell. The author, publisher, and all affiliates assume no responsibility for your trading results. There is a high risk in trading.

HYPOTHETICAL OR SIMULATED PERFORMANCE RESULTS HAVE CERTAIN LIMITATIONS. UNLIKE AN ACTUAL PERFORMANCE RECORD, SIMULATED RESULTS DO NOT REPRESENT ACTUAL TRADING. ALSO, SINCE THE TRADES HAVE NOT BEEN EXECUTED, THE RESULTS MAY HAVE UNDER-OR-OVER COMPENSATED FOR THE IMPACT, IF ANY, OF CERTAIN MARKET FACTORS, SUCH AS THE LACK OF LIQUIDITY. SIMULATED TRADING PROGRAMS IN GENERAL ARE ALSO SUBJECT TO THE FACT THAT THEY ARE DESIGNED WITH THE BENEFIT OF HINDSIGHT. NO REPRESENTATION IS BEING MADE THAT ANY ACCOUNT WILL OR IS LIKELY TO ACHIEVE PROFIT OR LOSSES SIMILAR TO THOSE SHOWN.

Made in the USA
Coppell, TX
21 August 2020